EUGENE ATGET

Eugène Atget

A selection of photographs from the
collection of the Musée Carnavalet, Paris

Introduction by Françoise Reynaud

PANTHEON BOOKS, NEW YORK

CENTRE NATIONAL DE LA PHOTOGRAPHIE, PARIS

On the cover: Corner, rue de Seine, 6th arrondissement c. 1924.

Library of Congress Cataloging in Publication Data

Atget, Eugène, 1856-1927.
Eugène Atget.

Bibliography: p.
1. Photography, Artistic.   2. Atget, Eugène, 1856-1927.
I. Reynaud, Françoise.   II. Title.
TR653.A83   1985   779'.092'4   85-42850
ISBN 0-394-74084-X (pbk.)

Manufactured in France

EXHIBITS
"These are only documents"

In the field of legend, a certain number of myths have grown up around the character and work of Eugène Atget (1857-1927). The most tenacious of these are that of the wandering, tramplike photographer, pushing a handcart through the streets of Paris, and that of the perfectly naïve individual who doesn't realize the value of his own work. He has also been described as a hawker of images who sold his prints on the terraces of the cafés in St-Germain-des-Prés for a song, or as a craftsman who said of his photographs: "These are only documents." This phrase, while being authentic, should be put into context.

Research has been carried out over the past few years and traces of him have been found in archives; public and private collections have kept thousands of his photos and there are accounts by witnesses who either knew him themselves or had been told stories about him. Thanks to this it is now possible to have a fair vision of things, even though this is rendered rather difficult by the complexity of Atget's character and works. However, in order to understand him better, we have to examine the different facets of the portrait which has been made of him since 1925.

Atget, a surrealist?

A few years before his death, he met up with the surrealists and in particular the painter Man Ray, whose studio was also in rue Campagne-Première at Montparnasse. The artists and writers of this avant-garde viewed his photographs in a very special way, finding in them a dimension that he himself had evidently not looked for. They published some of them in 1926 in their magazine *La Révolution surréaliste* to go with their ideas, but without mentioning his name as he had asked them not to, no doubt for fear of associating himself with their movement. It seems that certain of his photographs lent themselves to exercises in surrealist thought and after 1927 some exhibitions of surrealist photographs presented his works under his name. The ones which were shown in the important exhibitions in Stuttgart, Vienna and Berlin in 1929 and 1930 *(Film und Foto)* belonged to the American photographer Berenice Abbott. She was a student of Man Ray who, after Atget's death, had bought the negatives which had not been put in the Photographic Archives of Historical Monuments and also the photographs in his reference albums.

In fact, the surrealists especially liked those of Atget's works which could be reinterpreted, like the scene "The Eclipse," which they called "New Conversions" because the spectators grouped on place de la Bastille are all looking up at the sky. Or his shop windows, displays of goods, and the special things that happened in the streets and which he captured in his own way, searching for the most evocative angle which could best serve the needs of his clientele. Certain images revealed a total lack of reference to traditional conventions in framing and composition and an unusual interest in subjects which were not strictly "artistic." They portrayed the everyday environment with no embellishment whatsoever, and the realities with which one rubbed shoulders without noticing them. His world took on the appearance of a living dream and echoed the surrealist community's research into phenomena of the unconscious and its effect on creativity. These artists and intellectuals knew Atget as an old man who was not very talkative, perhaps embittered by not having published his work on Old Paris. He was in any case a very modest man, although he was always sure of what interested him. They described him as quite a wild, surly person, and unpretentious.

Some young photographers who were in Paris at that time, Berenice Abbott, Walker Evans, and Brassaï, evolved in the surrealist milieu and were strongly influenced not only by the composition of Atget's subjects, but also by the systematic way in which he portrayed a place.

Atget, a forerunner?

Ever since 1930 he has been presented by publications on the history of photography as a forerunner in 20th century research. This is quite a paradox, since his technique was old;

he used a wooden camera and printed on albumen paper which he toned with gold, and the subjects he chose were most often traditional.

In 1930 an article signed by Waldemar George was published in an issue of the magazine *Arts et Métiers graphiques* dedicated to photography. It proves that three years after his death, Atget was already considered a master: "Atget is a maniac, a solitary walker who collects views like museum pieces. In playing the role of a forerunner and creating works which we estimate as highly as those of Douanier Rousseau, Atget is only following his divination(...). These works break free from the fluctuations of sovereign fashion, like a Charlie Chaplin film or a painting by the Douanier Rousseau." The legend of Atget the "hawker" was also spoken about in this text.

At the same time, certain of his photographs were published. The anticonformist magazine *Le Crapouillot* chose in May 1929 to illustrate practically an entire issue on the history of Paris "with Atget's photograph album." It would probably have seemed only normal to Atget that his work should be used in this way. And in 1930 Jonquières, a publisher of art books, published a very beautiful book which came out in Paris, New York and Leipzig. Most of the ninety-six photographs chosen for it came from the collection of Berenice Abbott, who was working hard to distribute Atget's works. They still revealed to a large extent the taste of the surrealists with numerous disembodied views of Paris. The preface by Pierre Mac-Orlan consisted of reflections on photography in general and on Paris as a capital city and told us little about Atget, except that he was "cultured."

Around the 1930s, Atget's photographs were known mainly as a kind of dehumanized commentary on the town and its outskirts. What we now know of his works as a whole allows us to be more subtle than Walter Benjamin, who said in a text that later became famous: "The fortifications at Porte d'Arcueil are empty, the magnificent staircases are empty, the courtyards too are empty, terraces of cafés are empty, place du Tertre, suitably, is empty(...). The town is emptied like lodgings which have not yet found a new tenant. In works like these, surrealist photography is paving the way for this salutory movement which will make man and the world around him strangers to one another. From the politically educated point of view, it is opening a clear field where intimacy gives way to the lighting up of details." Walter Benjamin had discerned how this type of picture could be used: "For the evolution of history, those left behind by Atget are real exhibits." But as he only knew part of the works, he deformed Atget's approach: "We say quite rightly that he took photographs like one would take photographs of the scene of a crime(...). The picture taken has no other purpose than detecting the clues." Not all Atget's photographs are "empty." In eliminating, or dissimulating, human presence, his aim was to capture as truly as possible the essence of certain subjects, from streets, crossroads, façades of houses, to courtyards and bars. And it is exactly these *empty* images which have always struck the person looking at them the hardest. These photographs are striking, either because they are particularly asymmetrical because of sometimes even seeming to topple over, or, a great sense of balance in the lines, the forms and the plays of light. It goes without saying that they do not all – he took more than 8,500 between about 1890 and 1927 – have the same intensity. Many are "only documents," for Atget actually tried to respond to the needs and tastes of the clientele that he had built up gradually – a far cry from the surrealist approach which diverted the objects from their original destination. If he gathered "clues," it was primarily for commercial reasons, especially at the beginning of his work. But throughout his career he had a growing personal interest in art and history.

Another avant-garde group called *le Groupe des XV,* founded in 1945 in Paris and not as well known as the surrealists, was drawn to these photographs. On the occasion of their first exhibition Louis Chéronnet commented: "Today divested of vain aestheticism, photography has gone back to the style of the Nadars and the Atgets." For them the documentary aspect, the impression that many of his photos give of being a strict report, were the essence itself of "pure photography" as they meant to practise it. Sougez, who directed the photographic department of *L'Illustration* from 1920 until the war, had collaborated in 1930 in the publication of the special issue of *Arts et Métiers graphiques.* Marcel Bovis, and also Robert Doisneau, Willy Ronis and to a certain extent the Séeberger brothers and Pierre Jahan, claimed to be inspired by Atget's works or admitted affinities with his approach.

If the avant-gardes were the first to officially recognize Atget as a master, the photographic world follows suite, even though at times with a certain reticence. In his monumental history of photography which was published in 1945, Raymond Lécuyer has presented him both as a "forerunner" and a "wandering photographer," "knight errant of photography."

Atget, a continuator?

It has often been said that Atget's work has not been appreciated in his own country. It is certain that he was not talked about much around 1960 and 1970. Shortly afterwards the situation changed, thanks to renewed interest in the history of photography in general. Nowadays historians systematically turn their attention to the works of the XIXth and XXth century and try to explain, according to their different perspectives, the respective parts of personal creativity and historical determination. One can schematize by distinguishing an aesthetic tendency, which follows the rules of classical art history, and a historical tendency, which analyzes the social, political and economic problems linked to artistic production. Research carried out in both directions sometimes comes to contradictory conclusions.

This is sometimes the case with respect to Atget; hence certain polemics between those who wanted only to see a political meaning, and even intention, in his work, and those who look at it from a uniquely aesthetic point of view. In actual fact objective research carried out intelligently in one or other direction has turned up some complementary clarifications. We know for example that Atget had favourable opinions of the socialist and revolutionary movements at his epoch. It is also clear that certain themes such as courtyards, alleyways and solitary corners were born of his artistic sensitivity and brought us his most beautiful images.

After Jean Leroy, who prepared the ground for a more reliable biography, American researchers turned up some new aspects of Atget's personality and works. The Museum of Modern Art in New York acquired Berenice Abbott's collection in 1968 and this gave rise to deep studies of his life, his method of taking photographs, how he organized his work and his clientele. In France, museums and public collections have long been in possession of photographs, arranged in iconographic series with other documents. Their aim is to offer the largest possible range of information on every aspect of a subject. Each document, drawing, engraving or photograph represents a stage of artistic or historical evolution. The works of the great XIXth and XXth century photographers are only now beginning to be treated in a different manner: inventoried under the names of the photographers, they are grouped separately. Thus Atget's photos, which were mostly bought during his lifetime, are gradually being taken out of topographic and thematic series.

Atget had in fact began by making "documents for artists." He then became interested in Old Paris and, as actor André Calmettes wrote to Berenice Abbott in 1928, his ambition was to "create a collection of everything that was artistic or picturesque in Paris and its outskirts." Letters sent by Atget to the director of the Beaux-Arts in 1920, suggesting that they buy his negatives, reflect this concern; he writes of having recorded everything which bears witness to the past, everything which is typical, "picturesque." He paid particular attention to things which were going to disappear and sometimes put a note with the photographs saying "will disappear." Through his attachment to the "picturesque," he approaches the romantic trend of the first half of the XIXth century which was interested in antique and mediaeval remains of European architecture. Anxious to set down a portrait of Old Paris, he joined to those who, after Baron Haussmann's transformations of Paris from a medieval city into a modern town, were trying to react against the disappearance of its traditional characteristics. At the same moment he began taking photographs of Paris, the Commission of Old Paris was founded. He never worked for it, however, as he wanted to stay completely independent, but their photographers used to work in the same quarters as he did.

Taking into account all the innovations that Atget brought to the photography of his epoch, during which pictorialism was in full bloom, we have to admit that he was also a continuator. Beaumont Newhall had classified him as a documentary photographer because of the pictures he took of peddlers and rag-and-bone men, along with the sociological reports of Jacob August Riis and Lewis Hine, whom he had probably never seen. We should now rather link him up with the French photographers of the XIXth century, and it is likely that he saw certain of their pictures. Even if it is certain that he took very few photos by order (except at the beginning of his career, then a few other times, to photograph the Jardin des Tuileries for the Bibliothèque historique de la Ville de Paris, and some prostitutes for the painter Dignimont, not forgetting the views of Rouen which were possibly ordered by a collector), because of repeated contact with amateurs of Old Paris, curators and librarians, he was able to see what others had done before him. Some examples are the views of Henri Le Secq, who in 1852 took photographs of demolitions in Paris, or those of Charles Marville which were taken before and after the changes made by Haussmann.

There were, in any case, lots of images of every epoch in the books published at the beginning of the XXth century on the history of Paris. We know from the pictures that Atget took of the interior of his house that he liked engravings and books. He managed to sell some of his pictures to publishers. So he must be regarded as a continuator of ancient traditions. Are not his "small crafts" a prolongation of the drawings *Cris de Paris* by Boucher and Bouchardon, who in the XVIIIth century were already the heirs of a long-established style? And are not the *"veües"* engraved in the XVIIth century by a certain Israël Silvestre the ancestors of his views of Paris? The heading on his notepaper shows us his principal preoccupation: "Atget, author-publisher of « A Collection of Photographs of Old Paris » (Monuments and aspects), 17 bis, rue Campagne-Première, Paris XIVe."

Furthermore, it is very surprising that he never officially presented himself as a photographer. Administratively, he was registered as a "dramatic artist," his first profession, or "author-publisher," which enabled him to avoid buying a license. He was also a "lecturer," for he gave evening classes on theatre in the "Universités populaires" of certain districts of Paris from 1904-1913. The different ways in which he placed himself apart from photography are even more surprising because of the fact that he seemed to know very well what he was doing. When he said to Berenice Abbott: "People don't know what to photograph," to justify his refusal to take orders for photos, he was asserting a true awareness of the value of his work. He had worked out a remarkable filing system for his negatives and prints. He made albums to group and present his photographs by their theme: courtyards, doorknockers, decorative details, fortifications, interiors, etc. He noted information about his clientele very carefully; names and addresses of artists, craftsmen, decorators, illustrators, collectors, publishers and other potential buyers were accompanied by the themes which interested them and the prices he should ask each one to pay. His most famous clients were a few academic painters like Edouard Detaille or Luc Olivier Merson, and the Montparnasse artists, Man Ray, Foujita, Kisling, Braque and also Utrillo, Derain and Delaunay.

The souvenirs of certain people and the notes he made on his prints show that he organized his work according to the seasons and the time of day. "These are only documents," he replied to Man Ray when asked by him to get more up-to-date papers for his prints. Did he mean that photography itself, on which he had written nothing, didn't interest him? André Calmettes said: "He was absolute in art, in hygiene. He had his own ideas about everything, and he imposed them with incredible violence. He applied this intransigence of taste, vision and methods to the art of photography...". Falsely modest, had Atget convinced himself that his approach was the only right one? He had been an actor, he loved painting and painted a little, he was passionate about art and history. The photographs he took gave him the scope to express all that.

He progressed from the photos he took before 1900 to be used by painters, in which he gave priority to interesting patterns, plants, animals, objects, people, or details of architecture, to more general views, to town and country landscapes, and to things which characterized an epoch or a style. He always took the same care in the use of form, but at the same time tried to meet the needs of his clients, who were amateurs of Old Paris and of ancient French traditions. There were two reasons for the documentary character of his work: aesthetic and historic. He had to support the subjects and make them useful for the artists. This led to certain distortions which are not only due to technical problems; and the same images had to be used to illustrate the history of a place. Berenice Abbott wondered about the presence of reflections which any other photographer would have avoided. He didn't worry about a blurred or moving shape.

For a long time he produced "documents," probably because he never wanted to do anything else, but taking great care – and no doubt great pleasure also – to obtain arrangements which were more and more constructed, balanced or dynamic. Later, towards the end of his life, he adopted a more personal approach. Around the twenties, perhaps when commercial considerations were less urgent, he started expressing the atmosphere of places. His research in this direction led to the foggy views of certain corners of Paris and of the parc de Sceaux. These photos, which are full of poetry, still show two aspects, both expressed to their utmost degree. Firstly the documentary aspect, since *all* the aspects of a place had to be portrayed. And secondly the artistic intention, which flows directly from his works and makes us forget the utilitarian aspect.

Heritor of a historic and artistic tradition, Atget's work is also a new reflection of the image of a culture, perhaps because, in the end, his main concern went beyond the art of photography.

Françoise Reynaud
translation by Gill Bennett.

1. Corner of rue de Seine, Paris 6, about 1924.

2. Courtyard, 41 rue Broca, Paris 5, 1912.

3. Courtyard, 21 rue Mazarine, Paris 6, 1911.

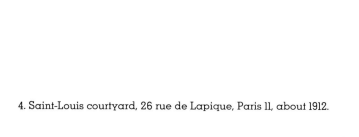

4. Saint-Louis courtyard, 26 rue de Lapique, Paris 11, about 1912.

5. Place Saint-André-des-Arts, Paris 6, about 1903-1904.

6. Cabaret de la Croix d'Or, 54 rue Saint-André-des-Arts, Paris 6, about 1900.

7. 178, rue de Choisy, Paris 13, about 1914.

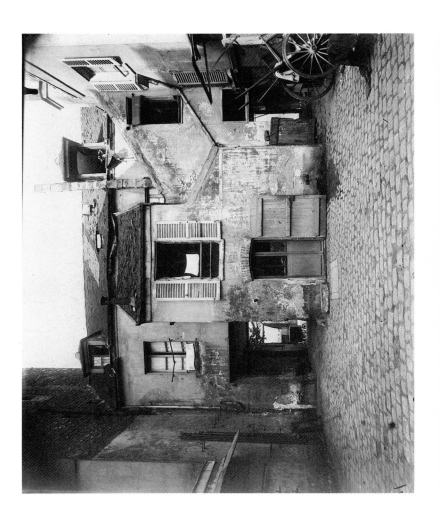

8. Ancient passage over Pont-Neuf, Paris 6, March 1913.

9. 7, rue de Valence, Paris 5, about 1922.

10. Courtyard, 8 rue Pavée, about 1911.

11. Porte d'Ivry, impasse Masséna, 18 and 20
boulevard Masséna, about 1907-1910.

12. Montmartre, 18 rue du Mont-Cenis, Paris 18, about 1921.

13. Cour de Rouen, Paris 19, 1915.

14. Parc Delessert, Paris 16, 1914.

15. Porte Maillot, fortifications, Paris 16, vers 1913.

16. Porte de Ménilmontant, Paris 20, fortifications, café, about 1910.

17. The Bièvre, boulevard d'Italie, Paris 13, obsolete since 1891.
Today called rue Edmond Gondinet.

18. Porte Dauphine, fortifications, Paris 16, about 1913.

19. Ruelle des Gobelins, Paris 13, about 1922.

20. The Point du Jour, Bas Meudon gate, on the quayside, boulevard Victor, Paris 15, about 1910.

21. Porte Maillot, fortifications, Paris 16, about 1913.

22. Entrance to courtyard, cour du Dragon on the
rue du Dragon, Paris 6, about 1912-1913.

23. Rue Eginhard, Paris 4, about 1900.

24. House, 50 rue de Turenne, Paris 3, about 1913.

25. Au petit Dunkerque, quai de Conti, Paris 3, 1900.

26. Group of children and painters, 1901.

3

27. Rue Mondétour, between rue de la Grande-Truanderie and rue Pirouette, Paris 1, 1908.

28. Inside a decorator's appartment, rue du Montparnasse,
Paris 6 or 14, 1910.

29. Rue du Maure, entrance to passage de la Réunion, Paris 3, 1908.

30. Corner, rue Vauvilliers, Paris 1, 1898.

31. The Halles Butcher's shop, Paris 1, about 1900.

32. Fish market, rue Mouffetard, Paris 5, 1898.

33. Little market, place Saint-Médard, Paris 5, 1898.

34. Billboard, colonne Morris place Denfert-Rochereau, Paris 14, 1898-1900.

35. Furniture removers, 1898-1900.

36. Rue Férou, Paris 6, about 1923.

37. Courtyard, 34 rue des Bourdonnais, Paris 1, 1908.

38. Milliner's interior, place Saint-André-des-Arts, Paris 6, 1910.

39. Courtyard of Hôtel de Beauvais, 68 rue François-Miron 4, about 1902.

40. Hôtel de La Monnaie Courtyard, quai Conti, Paris 6, 1905-1906.

41. Staircase, Hôtel de la Monnaie, quai Conti, Paris 6, about 1906-1907.

42. Austrian Embassy, 57 rue de Varenne, Paris 7, about 1905.

43. Hôtel du Président Talon, 73 rue de Grenelle, Paris 7, about 1909.

44. Hôtel du Maréchal de Tallard, 78 rue des Archives, Paris 3, about 1901-1912.

45. Saint-Séverin church, view from the rooftops, Paris 5, about 1903-1904.

46. La Monnaie lock, Pont-Neuf, Paris 6, about 1910.

47. Puppet show, Luxembourg gardens, Paris 6, 1899.

48. Corner, rue de la Montagne-Sainte-Geneviève, Paris 5, 1924.

49. Saint-Séverin church, view taken on the roof, Paris 5, about 1903-1904.

50. Porte de Gentilly, Paris 13, 1920-1927.

51. Porte de Gentilly, boulevard Kellermann, Paris 13, about 1910.

52. Passy, passage des Eaux, Paris 16, about 1901.

53. Moulin de la Galette, Montmartre, Paris 18, about 1900.

54. Ruelle des Gobelins, the Bièvre, Paris 13, about 1899.

55. Auberge du Compas d'or, 72 rue Montorgueil, Paris 2, about 1905.

56. Passage Sainte-Anne, 61 rue Sainte-Anne, Paris 2, about 1907.

57. Wine cellars at Bercy, Paris 12, about 1913.

58. Porte d'Asnières, passage Trébert, Paris 17,
rag-and-bone men about 1913.

59. Porte d'Ivry, Paris 13, courtyard of a rag-and-bone man, about 1910.

60. Porte d'Asnières, cité Valmy, Paris 17, rag-and-bone men, 1913.

61. Entrance to courtyard, 9 rue Thouin, Paris 5, about 1910.

BIOGRAPHY

1857. 12th February, Jean-Eugène-Auguste Atget is born in Libourne (Dordogne), of Jean-Eugène Atget, coach- builder, and Clara-Adeline Hourlier.

1859. The Atget family moves to Bordeaux and the father becomes a commercial traveller.

1862. The father dies in Paris; the mother dies shortly afterwards.

1862-1878. Eugène Atget is brought up by his maternal grandparents in Bordeaux. When he leaves school, Atget joins the Navy.

1878. He moves to Paris and tries unsuccessfully to be accepted by the Conservatoire national de Musique et d'Art dramatique to study acting. His national service begins (official duration: five years).

1879. Manages to be accepted by the Conservatoire and attends Edmond Got's classes. He lives at 50 rue Notre-Dame-de-Lorette at M. Eysserie's.

1881. He studies acting and does his national service at the same time, and fails his exams at the Conservatoire. His maternal grandparents die. Atget spends a year in a regiment in Tarbes.

1882. September: Atget is released from national service a year early and returns to Paris (12, rue des Beaux-Arts); he acts "third-rate roles" with a theatre group playing in the suburbs of Paris and in the provinces. He meets André Calmettes, who is to become and stay his friend, and mixes with painters.

1886. About this time he meets Valentine Compagnon (born in 1847); she acts too, and will live with him until she dies in 1926. She had an illegitimate son (1878-1914) who had a son himself called Valentin Compagnon. Atget and Valentine Compagnon had no children.

1887. A throat infection forces Atget to leave the theatre.

1888. Approximate date when Atget moves to a region called la Somme; this is probably when he begins taking photos.

1890. Return to Paris (5 rue de la Pitié); Atget abandons painting – although he will always paint a little – and decides to become a professional photographer. He writes on his door "Documents for artists" and puts an advertisement in *La Revue des Beaux-Arts* in February 1892 describing his work: "...landscapes, animals, flowers, monuments, documents, foregrounds for artists, copies of pictures, can travel. Collection for private circulation only."

1897. Begins taking his views of Paris, always in the old quarters. Begins the series called "Small Crafts in Paris" which is used to make a series of 80 postcards by the publisher V. Porcher.

1898. Atget sells his first photographs to public collections.

1899. He moves to 17 bis rue Campagne-Première in Montparnasse where he will live until he dies.

1901. Starts photographing door knockers, the outskirts of Paris, and "Art in Old Paris."

1901-1902. Starts working on details of the decoration on façades of houses, balconies, doors, etc.

1903-1904. Starts working on courtyards, staircases and the inside and outside of churches.

1904-1913. Atget lectures on the theatre in the "Universités populaires."

1905-1906. Starts working on staircases, fireplaces, and the inside of "hotels" from the old regime.

Around 1907. He agrees to photograph the centre of town for the Bibliothèque historique de Paris.

1910. He begins selling his home-made albums to the musée Carnavalet and the Bibliothèque nationale.

1911-1912. He donates a collection of socialist political newspapers to the Bibliothèque historique de la Ville de Paris.

1914. Atget gradually stops taking photographs.

1917. He sells newspaper articles on the Dreyfus affair, which he has been collecting since 1896, to the Bibliothèque nationale.

1917-1918. He stores his negatives in the cellar of his house to protect them from German bombs.

1919. He takes photographs again of Paris and the outskirts.

1920. Writes letters to Paul Léon, director of the Beaux-Arts, offering to sell his collection on art in Old Paris and picturesque Paris. Sells 2621 negatives for 10,000 Francs (today they are in the Archives photographiques de la Direction du Patrimoine).

1921. Takes photographs of prostitutes for the painter André Dignimont.

1925. He photographs the parc de Sceaux.

1926. Valentine Compagnon dies.

1927. Eugène Atget dies on August 4th. His friend André Calmettes probably takes care of his estate. Les Archives photographiques d'Art et d'Histoire buy about 2000 negatives which they have kept. The photographer Berenice Abbott buys the remaining negatives and prints.

BIBLIOGRAPHY

Books

Atget photographe de Paris, preface by Pierre MacOrlan, Paris, Jonquières, 1930; American edition, New York, Weyhe, 1930; German edition: **Eugène Atget, Lichtbilder,** preface by Camille Recht, Paris and Leipzig, 1930. 96 photographs.

Saint-Germain-des-Prés 1900 vu par Atget, by Yvan Christ, published by "Comité de la quinzaine de Saint-Germain," Paris 1951.

Eugène Atget by Berenice Abbott, Prague 1963.

A vision of Paris, The Photographs of Eugène Atget, The Words of Marcel Proust, Arthur D. Trottenberg, New York, MacMillan Publishing, 1963; French edition: **Paris du temps perdu: photographies d'Eugène Atget, textes de Marcel Proust,** Lausanne, Edita, Paris, Bibliothèque des Arts, 1963. 118 photographs of Paris and outskirts from Berenice Abbott's collection.

The World of Atget by Berenice Abbott, New York 1964; republished in New York, Paragon Books, G.P. Putman's Sons, 1979. 176 photos.

Atget, magicien du Vieux Paris, by Jean Leroy, Joinville-le-Pont, Pierre-Jean Balbo, 1975. First monography on Atget in French. 72 photographs.

Eugène Atget Lichtbilder, text by Gabriele Forberg, preface by Camille Recht, postface by Dietrich Leube, Munich, Rogner und Bernhard, 1975.

Eugène Atget, voyages en ville, text by Romeo Martinez, Pierre Gassmann and Alain Pougetoux, Paris, Chêne and Hachette, 1979: Italian edition.

Milan, Electa Editrice, 1979, 129 photographs.

Eugène Atget, text by Ben Lisson, New York, Aperture, "The Aperture History of Photography Series," 1980.

The Work of Atget, John Szarkowski and Maria Morris Hambourg. 4 volumes published by the Museum of Modern Art of New York, 1981-1985.
Vol. 1: **Old France,** 1981, 121 plates and 83 small reproductions, "Atget and the Art of Photography" by J. Szarkowski, notices by M. Morris Hambourg.
Vol 2: **The Art of Old Paris,** 1982, 117 plates and 95 small reproductions, "A biography of Eugène Atget" and notes by M. Morris Hambourg.
Vol 3: **The Ancien Régime,** 1983, 120 plates and 47 small reproductions, "The Structure of the Work" by M. Morris Hambourg. Notes by J. Szarkowski.
Vol. 4: **Modern Times,** 117 plates and 88 small reproductions, "Understandings of Atget," by John Szarkowski.

Eugène Atget, 1857-1927, by James Borcoman, National Gallery of Canada, Ottawa, 1984.

Eugène Atget, texts by Romeo Martinez and Ferdinand Sciana, Milan, Fabbri, I Grandi Fotografi, 1982, Paris, Photo, Les Grands Maîtres de la Photographie, 1984, 69 photos.

Unpublished Theses

Eugène Atget 1857-1927, The Structure of the Work, Maria Morris Hambourg, Ph. D. Thesis, Columbia University, 1980.

Atget's Seven Albums in practice, Margaret Nesbit, Ph. D. Thesis, Yale University, 1983.

Filmography

Eugène Atget Photographer,
Peter Wyeth, in colour, 16 mm, 50 mn,
Arts Council of Great Britain, 1982.

Articles

Desnos, Robert, "Emile Atget" (sic),
Merle, N° 3, May 1929, unsigned,
reproduced in **Nouvelles-Hébrides
et autres textes,** 1922-1930, Paris,
Gallimard, 1978, p. 435 onwards.

Abbott, Berenice, "Eugène Atget,"
Creative Art, vol. 5, N° 3, September
1929, p. 651-656.

Fels, Florent, "Atget," **L'Art vivant,** N° 7,
February 1931, p. 28.

Abbott, Berenice, "Eugène Atget,
Forerunner of Modern Photography"
U.S. Camera, vol. 1, N° 12, autumn
1940, p. 20-23, 48-49, 75.

Abbott, Berenice, "Eugène Atget"
Complete photographer, N° 6, 1941,
p. 335-339.

Leroy, Jean, "Eugène Atget qui étiez-
vous?," **Camera,** vol. 41, N° 12,
December 1962, p. 6-8, republished in
Camera, vol. 57, N° 3, March 1978,
p. 40-42.

Leroy, Jean, "Atget et son temps," **Terre
d'Images,** N° 3, May 1964, p. 357-372.

Brassaï, Gyula Halasz, "My Memories
of E. Atget, P.H. Emerson, and
Alfred Stieglitz," **Camera,** vol. 48, N° 1,
January 1969, p. 4-13, 21, 27, 37,

Szarkowski, John, "Atget," **Album,** N° 3,
April 1970.

Fraser, John, "Atget and the City,"
Studio International, vol. 182,
December 1971.

Lemagny, Jean-Claude, "Le Bonhomme
Atget," **Photo,** N° 87, December 1974.

Hill, Paul and Tom Cooper, "Interview
Man Ray," **Camera,** vol. 54, N° 2,
February 75, p. 37-40.

Johnson, William, "Eugène Atget.
A Chronological Bibliography,"
Exposure, May 1977, p. 13-15.

Gautrand, Jean-Claude, "Atget,"
Le Nouveau Photo Cinéma, N° 62,
November 1977.

Camera, N° 3, March 1978, special
issue on Atget. Texts by Romeo Martinez,
Alain Pougetoux and Jean Leroy.

Leroy, Jean, "La vérité sur Atget,"
Camera, volume 58, N° 11, November
1979, p. 15, 41-42.

Michaels, Barbara, "An Introduction
to the Dating and Organisation of
Eugène Atget's photographs," **The Art
Bulletin,** vol. 61, September 1979,
p. 460-468.

Pougetoux, Alain, "A photographer,
a town: Atget and Rouen." **Monuments
Historiques,** N° 110, 1980.

Hellman, Roberta and Marvin
Hoshino, "On the Rationalization of
Eugène Atget," **Arts Magazine,**
February 1982.

Starenko, Michael, "The Work of Atget:
Old France," **Afterimage,** vol. 9, N° 7,
February 1982, p. 6 and 7.

Badger, Gerry, "Atget and the Garden
of Critical Delights," **The Photographic
Collector,** vol. 3, N° 1, spring 1983,
p.41-43.

Pougetoux, Alain, "Intérieurs parisiens,"
et Reynaud, Françoise, "The Work of
Atget," **Photographies,** n° 1, printemps
1983, p. 102-110.

EXHIBITIONS

1928. "Premier Salon des Indépendants de la Photographie," Comédie des Champs-Elysées, main staircase, Paris (photographs by Atget probably belonging to Man Ray, together with those of Germaine Krull, André Kertész, Man Ray, Paul Outerbridge and other avant-garde photographers).

1929-1930. "Film und Foto," 1929, Stuttgart (11 of Atget's photos belonging to Berenice Abbott); 1930, Vienna (5 of Atget's photos).

1930. Berlin.

1930. "Atget," Weyhe Gallery, New York (the gallery where Julien Levy worked; exhibition coincided with the publication of the English edition of the book prefaced by Pierre MacOrlan "Eugène Atget, Parisian photographer."

1931. "Nadar and Atget, Old French Photographers," Julien Levy Gallery, New York.

1932. "Surrealism," Julien Levy Gallery, New York (a few of Atget's photos were exposed).

1939. "Eugène Atget," Photo-League, New York.

1940. "Clarence John Laughlin," Julien Levy Gallery, New York (photographs of New Orleans compared with photographs of Paris by Eugène Atget).

1941. "Vues de Paris et petits métiers," photographs by Marville, Atget, and Vert, musée Carnavalet, Paris.

1965. "A century of photography, from Nièpce to Man Ray," musée des Arts Décoratifs, Paris (28 photographs by Atget).

1972. "Hommage à Atget, Denis Brihat," 2 simultaneous exhibitions, Galerie La Demeure, Paris (27 photographs by Atget).

1972. "Eugène Atget," Museum of Modern Art, New York.

1978. "Eugène Atget, Das Alte Paris," Rheinisches Landesmuseum, Bonn, 79 photographs, catalogue.

1978. "Eugene Atget, photographer," 1857-1927, travelling exhibition in France, modern prints done by Pictorial Service from negatives of Archives photographiques de la Direction de l'Architecture, (79 photographs, illustrated catalogue, text by Alain Pougetoux).

1979. "Atget's Gardens, a selection of Eugène Atget's photographs," London (R.I.B.A.), New York (I.C.P.), Washington (I.E.F.), (77 photographs, catalogue, text by William Howard Adams).

1981. "Atget," Galerie Zur Stockeregg, Zurich (56 photographs, illustrated catalogue, text by Hans Georg Puttnies).

1981. "Hommage à Atget," Troisième Triennale de la Photographie de Fribourg, Switzerland (no catalogue, 47 photographs with the theme "Reflections").

1981-1984. "The Work of Atget," four travelling exhibitions organized in the United States by the Museum of Modern Art of New York: 1981, "Old France"; 1982, "The Art of Old Paris"; 1983, "The Ancien Régime"; 1984, "Modern Times" (four books published in coordination with the exhibitions).

1982. "Eugène Atget, Intérieurs parisiens artistiques, pittoresques et bourgeois, début du XXe siècle," Mois de la Photo, musée Carnavalet, Paris (61 photographs, illustrated catalogue, texts by Margaret Nesbit and Françoise Reynaud).
On show in 1983 in Malmö, Sweden, the exhibition of originals and their reproductions is at present going round American universities.

ATGET'S PHOTOGRAPHIC TECHNIQUE

Atget used a wooden, swivelling bellows camera, measuring 18 x 24 cm, for horizontal or vertical shots, with a rectilinear lens. The inverted image was formed on the glass focusing screen at the back of the camera. The centring and focusing were done under the black cloth. The time of exposure and the weight of his equipment meant that he had to use a wooden support. Atget carried with him a certain number of negative plates in frames which could be adapted to the room (in a photo taken at the Austrian Embassy, now Hotel Matignon, we can see his camera reflected in a mirror). We know that he refused to use a more modern camera, in particular the one offered to him by Man Ray.

His negatives were glass plates measuring 18 x 24 cm with gelatino-silver bromide, bought in shops. When the development was finished, he varnished his plates. This varnish has often turned yellow.

Most of the photos are printed on albumen paper which he either bought ready to use or which he had to sensitize himself. The ready-to-use papers had the disadvantage of rapidly losing their qualities. Atget developed his photos in printing frames, contact print, in natural light. It is the direct darkening procedure which produces a very fine silver grain and consequently a very clear image and remarkably precise details. He sometimes carried out the exposure to light on his balcony. He then toned the prints, generally with gold, fixed and washed them, probably in his kitchen or in another room with running water. This is perhaps why there are certain imperfections which make it difficult to keep them in good condition. At the end of his life, Atget also used arrowroot papers (papers salted with starch) and gelatino-silver chloride papers. He toned the former with gold or platinum and the latter with gold. These latter ones were often particularly badly washed and so are now rather spoilt.

Atget's proofs were made in two different ways:
1. He would stick them on to grey-blue cardboard, very rarely on to beige paper; sometimes he varnished the proof. He wrote the legend on the mounting of the photograph, then the date and his signature.
2. They were fixed, but not stuck, in albums which he made himself, by sliding the four corners into slits. The clients could thus take the photos straight away and Atget hurriedly redeveloped them to fill up the empty pages. The albums were classified according to their themes. Atget wrote the legend and the number of the negative in pencil on the back of the proof and on the page of the album. He also sometimes put his rubber-stamped name and address on the back of the proof.

Atget made some cardboard albums with the proofs glued in for the collections of the Bibliothèque nationale. In the same way he made a dummy of a book "L'Art dans le Vieux Paris" ("Art in Old Paris") which is now in the Museum of Modern Art in New York.

PUBLIC COLLECTIONS
WHICH HAVE ATGET'S WORKS

The negatives:
Archives photographiques de la Direction du Patrimoine, fort de Saint-Cyr: a stock of several thousand glass plates, put together in 1920 when Atget offered to sell 2621 photos ("Art in Old Paris and Picturesque Paris"), and after his death by the acquisition of 2000 photos (Paris and outskirts).
The Museum of Modern Art of New York: about 1300 negatives from Berenice Abbott's collection.

Photographs in France:

● Bibliothèque nationale: thousands of photos sold by Atget between 1900 and 1927, albums.

● Bibliothèque historique de la Ville de Paris: 5655 photos bought between 1898 and 1914.

● Bibliothèque de l'Ecole nationale des Beaux-Arts: 1663 photos bought between 1900 and 1913.

● Bibliothèque du Musée des Arts Décoratifs: 1600 photos bought between 1900 and 1925.

● Fondation Doucet: 1600 photos.

● Bibliothèque de l'Arsenal: an album with 294 photos.

● Musée Carnavalet: about 2300 photos bought between 1898 and 1927, 18 albums, 3600 photos bought in 1952.

● Musée des Monuments Français.

● Musée du XIXᵉ siècle, Musée d'Orsay:

about fifty photos given by the Archives photographiques de la Direction du Patrimoine; and some bought in 1981.

● Musée Bricart, private museum of locks; 92 photos bought around 1904 by the Bricart brothers.

● Musée de l'Ile-de-France, château de Sceaux: about 700 photos being part of a stock at the Musée Carnavalet.

● Bibliothèque municipale de la Ville de Rouen: 50 photos bought in 1952

Photographs in other countries:

● United States: many museums have Atget's photos, the main ones being the Museum of Modern Art of New York (about 4000 photos from Berenice Abbott's collection, albums and address book), and George Eastman House in Rochester (photos from Man Ray's collection).

● England: photos bought from Atget, Victoria and Albert Museum, London.

THE ABBOTT-LEVY COLLECTION
AT THE MUSEUM OF MODERN ART IN NEW YORK

Berenice Abbott was born in 1898. American, she came to Paris in 1921 and again in 1923, after a visit to Berlin, to study sculpture. However, she was more interested in photography and became the student and assistant of Man Ray whose studio was at 31 rue Campagne-Première, near to Atget's home which was number 17 bis of the same street. Man Ray knew Atget and had some of his photographs. As from 1925, Berenice Abbott, like other artists in the surrealist circle and young Americans visiting Paris, bought some of Atget's photographs. In 1926 she opened her own studio of portrait photography; the two photos she took of Atget date from 1927. Immediately after Atget's death she wanted to buy everything she could: negatives, albums, photos, and the "address-book" where he noted the names and addresses of his clients, the time of day when he could go and see them, the subjects which interested them, the person who had recommended them, and the nearest metro station.

Julien Levy, an American whom Berenice Abbott had met through Man Ray and who was on the road to becoming an art dealer, helped her to buy her collection. We do not really know who received payment for it and Julien Levy wanted to remain anonymous. He let Berenice Abbott look after the collection and do lecture tours on Atget in Europe and the United States. She lent some photos to the exhibition *Film und Foto* (1929) and found publishers in Paris, Leipzig and New York to publish the book "Atget, the Photographer of Paris."

In 1964 she published "The World of Atget" in New York and published articles on Atget in magazines. She made prints from the Atget's negatives she had, marking them with a special stamp so they would not get muddled up with the ones that Atget had made himself. In 1968 the Museum of Modern Art in New York bought Berenice Abbott's collection and started doing methodical research into Atget's works.

PANTHEON PHOTO LIBRARY

The Pantheon Photo Library:
a collection conceived and produced by the
National Center of Photography in Paris
under the direction of Robert Delpire.